RUBANK EDUCATIONAL
LIBRARY No. 294

ONLINE MEDIA INCLUDED
Audio Recordings
Printable Piano Accompaniments

T0085035

# Concert and Contest COLLECTION

## *for* BARITONE B.C.

with piano accompaniment

Compiled and Edited

by  H. VOXMAN

**PLAYBACK+**
Speed • Pitch • Balance • Loop

To access recordings and PDF accompaniments visit:
**www.halleonard.com/mylibrary**

7285-9602-7795-6676

ISBN 978-1-4234-7729-7

RUBANK®

HAL•LEONARD®
7777 W. BLUEMOUND RD. P.O. BOX 13819 MILWAUKEE, WI 53213

Visit Hal Leonard Online at
**www.halleonard.com**

# Sarabanda and Gavotta

Baritone 𝄢

A. CORELLI
Edited by H. Voxman

# Dedication
### (Zueignung)

Baritone 𝄢

RICHARD STRAUSS, Op. 10, No. 1
Transcribed by H. Voxman

# Premier Solo de Concours

Baritone 𝄢

RENÉ MANIET
Edited by H. Voxman

# Calm As the Night

Baritone

CARL BÖHM
Edited by H. Voxman

# Andante and Allegro

Baritone 𝄢

ROBERT CLÉRISSE
Edited by H. Voxman

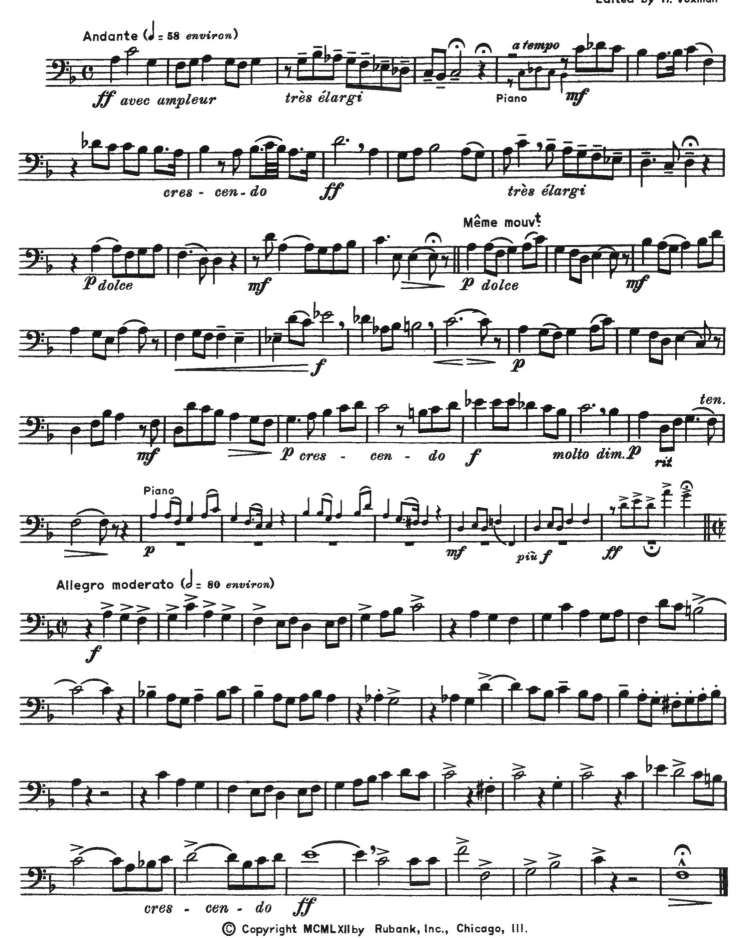

# Romance in E♭

**Baritone** 𝄢

LEROY OSTRANSKY

# Air Gai

Baritone 𝄢

G. P. BERLIOZ
Edited by H. Voxman

Baritone 𝄢

# Orientale

Baritone 𝄢

J. Ed. BARAT
Edited by H. Voxman

# Élégie

**Baritone** 𝄢

ALEXANDRE J. DUQUESNE
Edited by H. Voxman

# Serenade

**Baritone** 𝄢

OSKAR BÖHME, Op. 22, No. 1
Edited by H. Voxman

# My Regards

**Baritone** ♯:

EDWARD LLEWELLYN
Edited by H. Voxman

# L'Allegro
## (The Merry Man)

**Baritone ?:**

PAUL KOEPKE

# Petite Pièce Concertante

Baritone 𝄢

GUILLAUME BALAY
Edited by H. Voxman

# Morceau de Concours

**Baritone**

G. ALARY, Op. 57
Edited by H. Voxman

Baritone 𝄢

# Concertino

**Baritone** 𝄢

LEROY OSTRANSKY

# Andante
## from Concerto in Eb

**Baritone**

F. J. HAYDN
Edited by H. Voxman